POKÉMON™

MAD LIBS®

by Eric Luper

Mad Libs
An Imprint of Penguin Random House

MAD LIBS
Penguin Young Readers Group
An Imprint of Penguin Random House LLC

Mad Libs format copyright © 2017 by Penguin Random House LLC. All rights reserved.

Concept created by Roger Price & Leonard Stern

© 2017 The Pokémon Company International. ©1995–2017 Nintendo / Creatures Inc. / GAME
FREAK inc. TM, ®, and character names are trademarks of Nintendo.

Published by Mad Libs,
an imprint of Penguin Random House LLC,
345 Hudson Street, New York, New York 10014.
Printed in the USA.

ISBN 9781524785994
19

MAD LIBS® is a game for people who don't like games! It can be played by one, two, three, four, or forty.

• RIDICULOUSLY SIMPLE DIRECTIONS

In this tablet you will find stories containing blank spaces where words are left out. One player, the READER, selects one of these stories. The READER does not tell anyone what the story is about. Instead, he/she asks the other players, the WRITERS, to give him/her words. These words are used to fill in the blank spaces in the story.

• TO PLAY

The READER asks each WRITER in turn to call out a word—an adjective or a noun or whatever the space calls for—and uses them to fill in the blank spaces in the story. The result is a MAD LIBS® game.

When the READER then reads the completed MAD LIBS® game to the other players, they will discover that they have written a story that is fantastic, screamingly funny, shocking, silly, crazy, or just plain dumb—depending upon which words each WRITER called out.

• EXAMPLE (*Before* and *After*)

" _____ !" he said _____
          EXCLAMATION   ADVERB

as he jumped into his convertible _____ and
                                              NOUN

drove off with his _____ wife.
                            ADJECTIVE

"   **OUCH**   !" he said   **STUPIDLY**
          EXCLAMATION   ADVERB

as he jumped into his convertible   **CAT**   and
                                              NOUN

drove off with his   **BRAVE**   wife.
                            ADJECTIVE

In case you have forgotten what adjectives, adverbs, nouns, and verbs are, here is a quick review:

An ADJECTIVE describes something or somebody. *Lumpy*, *soft*, *ugly*, *messy*, and *short* are adjectives.

An ADVERB tells how something is done. It modifies a verb and usually ends in "ly." *Modestly*, *stupidly*, *greedily*, and *carefully* are adverbs.

A NOUN is the name of a person, place, or thing. *Sidewalk*, *umbrella*, *bridle*, *bathtub*, and *nose* are nouns.

A VERB is an action word. *Run*, *pitch*, *jump*, and *swim* are verbs. Put the verbs in past tense if the directions say PAST TENSE. *Ran*, *pitched*, *jumped*, and *swam* are verbs in the past tense.

When we ask for A PLACE, we mean any sort of place: a country or city (*Spain*, *Cleveland*) or a room (*bathroom*, *kitchen*).

An EXCLAMATION or SILLY WORD is any sort of funny sound, gasp, grunt, or outcry, like *Wow!*, *Ouch!*, *Whomp!*, *Ick!*, and *Gadzooks!*

When we ask for specific words, like a NUMBER, a COLOR, an ANIMAL, or a PART OF THE BODY, we mean a word that is one of those things, like *seven*, *blue*, *horse*, or *head*.

When we ask for a PLURAL, it means more than one. For example, *cat* pluralized is *cats*.

MAD LIBS® is fun to play with friends, but you can also play it by yourself! To begin with, DO NOT look at the story on the page below. Fill in the blanks on this page with the words called for. Then, using the words you have selected, fill in the blank spaces in the story.

Now you've created your own hilarious MAD LIBS® game!

SO, YOU WANT TO TRAIN POKÉMON?

VERB _____

ADJECTIVE _____

A PLACE _____

VERB ENDING IN "ING" _____

VERB _____

PLURAL NOUN _____

CELEBRITY _____

ADJECTIVE _____

NOUN _____

OCCUPATION _____

ADJECTIVE _____

NOUN _____

MAD☺LIBS®
SO, YOU WANT TO TRAIN POKÉMON?

So, you want to _____ Pokémon, huh? Well, it's not as
          VERB

_____ as it seems. First off, you'll need to find them. You can
ADJECTIVE

catch Pokémon in the wild or in (the) _____. Once you have
                                         A PLACE

a Charizard or a Blastoise, you'll need to gain its trust. That's not always

easy. You can try feeding it or _____ it, but the best
                     VERB ENDING IN "ING"

way to gain a Pokémon's trust is to _____ with it. Once you
                                   VERB

and your Pokémon are best _____, start training. You can
                          PLURAL NOUN

do this with a friend or even with _____ at a/an _____
                             CELEBRITY   ADJECTIVE

Gym nearby. Think of it like training a/an _____! Only when
                                   NOUN

you've trained enough should you challenge another _____
                                       OCCUPATION

for real. After all that work, it would be _____ for someone to
                               ADJECTIVE

come along and take your _____ away!
                        NOUN

MAD LIBS® is fun to play with friends, but you can also play it by yourself! To begin with, DO NOT look at the story on the page below. Fill in the blanks on this page with the words called for. Then, using the words you have selected, fill in the blank spaces in the story.

Now you've created your own hilarious MAD LIBS® game!

ASH'S PIKACHU!

ADJECTIVE _____

ADJECTIVE _____

NOUN _____

COLOR _____

NUMBER _____

PART OF THE BODY _____

ADJECTIVE _____

SILLY WORD _____

PERSON IN ROOM _____

PLURAL NOUN _____

VERB _____

PLURAL NOUN _____

ADJECTIVE _____

VERB _____

PERSON IN ROOM _____

MAD LIBS®

ASH'S PIKACHU!

I'm sure you've heard of Pikachu, Ash's _____ Pokémon. Like
                                          ADJECTIVE

most Pikachu, it has a plump, _____ body with a red
                                ADJECTIVE

_____ on each cheek. It has _____ tips on its ears
NOUN   COLOR

and _____ stripes on its _____. Ash's Pikachu may
      NUMBER   PART OF THE BODY

have evolved from a/an _____ Pichu, and could evolve (if it
                          ADJECTIVE

wanted) into a Raichu, which is quite like a/an _____. But
                                                  SILLY WORD

Ash's Pikachu likes itself just as it is. Professor _____ gave
                                                      PERSON IN ROOM

Pikachu to Ash when he was ten, and they've been best _____
                                                          PLURAL NOUN

ever since. Even though Pikachu is very cute, it can also _____
                                                            VERB

really well. Using the power of electricity, Pikachu can do all sorts of

_____ to defeat other Pokémon in battle. Some of its
PLURAL NOUN

_____ moves include Thunder Shock, Iron Tail, and
ADJECTIVE

_____! So, Rockruff, Bounsweet, or _____: You'd
VERB   PERSON IN ROOM

better watch out. Pikachu is here! Pika-pika!

MAD LIBS® is fun to play with friends, but you can also play it by yourself! To begin with, DO NOT look at the story on the page below. Fill in the blanks on this page with the words called for. Then, using the words you have selected, fill in the blank spaces in the story.

Now you've created your own hilarious MAD LIBS® game!

MY PERFECT POKÉMON BATTLE

ADJECTIVE _____

VERB ENDING IN "ING" _____

TYPE OF FOOD _____

ADJECTIVE _____

VERB _____

PERSON IN ROOM _____

VERB ENDING IN "ING" _____

ADJECTIVE _____

VERB _____

NOUN _____

ADJECTIVE _____

ADVERB _____

VERB _____

NOUN _____

VERB _____

PLURAL NOUN _____

A PLACE _____

NOUN _____

MAD LIBS®
MY PERFECT
POKÉMON BATTLE

The _____ seats are full. The crowd is _____
    ADJECTIVE   VERB ENDING IN "ING"

loudly. I have a/an _____ in my hand. And I'm ready to
                      TYPE OF FOOD

watch the most _____ Pokémon battle of all time! In my
                    ADJECTIVE

perfect battle, Ash would let Pikachu _____ the charge, while
                              VERB

_____ would be using Turtonator. Turtonator would start by
PERSON IN ROOM

_____ fire from its nostrils, but Pikachu is way too
VERB ENDING IN "ING"

_____! Pikachu would dodge to the left and _____
   ADJECTIVE   VERB

to the right! Then Pikachu would blast Turtonator with Static, making

Turtonator feel like a limp _____. Watch out! Next, Pikachu
                      NOUN

goes on a/an _____ attack. Pikachu would _____ use
            ADJECTIVE   ADVERB

Thunder Shock to _____ Turtonator, and Turtonator would
                    VERB

fall to the _____. The crowd would _____ louder
          NOUN   VERB

and louder until it felt like the whole stadium was going to collapse

into a pile of _____! No matter who you were rooting for,
          PLURAL NOUN

everyone would leave (the) _____ feeling like it was a/an
                        A PLACE

_____ worth watching!
   NOUN

MAD LIBS® is fun to play with friends, but you can also play it by yourself! To begin with, DO NOT look at the story on the page below. Fill in the blanks on this page with the words called for. Then, using the words you have selected, fill in the blank spaces in the story.

Now you've created your own hilarious MAD LIBS® game!

ASH KETCHUM, RENOWNED TRAINER!

NUMBER _____

ADVERB _____

ADJECTIVE _____

PERSON IN ROOM _____

PLURAL NOUN _____

NOUN _____

ADJECTIVE _____

ADVERB _____

PLURAL NOUN _____

NOUN _____

A PLACE _____

VERB _____

PLURAL NOUN _____

ADJECTIVE _____

ADJECTIVE _____

PLURAL NOUN _____

OCCUPATION _____

MAD LIBS
ASH KETCHUM, RENOWNED TRAINER!

Ash Ketchum started training Pokémon when he was only _____

NUMBER

years old. He might have been _____ young, but he was

ADVERB

_____! Early on, Ash became great friends with Misty and

ADJECTIVE

_____, but since then, he has traveled with lots of other

PERSON IN ROOM

_____. What Ash doesn't have in _____, he

PLURAL NOUN   NOUN

makes up for with his _____ friendships. His Pokémon fight

ADJECTIVE

extra _____ for him, and it shows. Even after many

ADVERB

_____, Team _____ has not been able to take

PLURAL NOUN   NOUN

Pikachu from Ash. Ash travels from Gym to _____ trying to

A PLACE

_____ Gym badges. Of course, along the way he solves

VERB

_____ and catches _____ Pokémon with his

PLURAL NOUN   ADJECTIVE

seemingly endless supply of Poké Balls. Through _____ work

ADJECTIVE

and long _____, Ash Ketchum plans to be the greatest

PLURAL NOUN

_____ ever!

OCCUPATION

MAD LIBS® is fun to play with friends, but you can also play it by yourself! To begin with, DO NOT look at the story on the page below. Fill in the blanks on this page with the words called for. Then, using the words you have selected, fill in the blank spaces in the story.

Now you've created your own hilarious MAD LIBS® game!

IF I WERE BOSS OF A POKÉMON GYM

ADJECTIVE _____

NOUN _____

A PLACE _____

COLOR _____

COLOR _____

VERB _____

PLURAL NOUN _____

ADVERB _____

NUMBER _____

NOUN _____

ADJECTIVE _____

NOUN _____

MAD LIBS®
IF I WERE BOSS OF A POKÉMON GYM

If I ran a Pokémon Gym, it would be the best _____ Gym in
ADJECTIVE

the world. We'd specialize in Fire-type Pokémon, but there would be

lots of other types there, too, like Flying types, Water types, and

_____ types. Let me tell you about it. My Gym would be in
NOUN

(the) _____ and the walls would be painted _____
A PLACE   _COLOR_

with _____ stripes. There would be places to battle, to rest,
COLOR

and of course, a place to _____. You'd never be bored there.
VERB

The Gym would be a place where all Trainers could come sharpen their

_____, while Pokémon could come to _____
PLURAL NOUN   _ADVERB_

gain experience by training _____ hours every day. But beware.
NUMBER

If you decide to challenge me to a/an _____, you'll lose. There
NOUN

has never been a Gym Leader as powerful or _____ as me.
ADJECTIVE

Enter at your own _____!
NOUN

MAD LIBS® is fun to play with friends, but you can also play it by yourself! To begin with, DO NOT look at the story on the page below. Fill in the blanks on this page with the words called for. Then, using the words you have selected, fill in the blank spaces in the story.

Now you've created your own hilarious MAD LIBS® game!

MEET TEAM ROCKET

VERB _____

VERB _____

A PLACE _____

ADJECTIVE _____

ADVERB _____

PART OF THE BODY _____

NOUN _____

ADJECTIVE _____

CELEBRITY _____

NOUN _____

ADJECTIVE _____

VERB _____

ADJECTIVE _____

VERB ENDING IN "ING" _____

COLOR _____

NOUN _____

MAD LIBS®

MEET TEAM ROCKET

If you're going to train and _____ Pokémon, you'd better
_____ VERB

know about Team Rocket. Team Rocket's goal is to _____
_____ VERB

Pokémon for profit and to gain domination in (the) _____.
_____ A PLACE

Although there are many members, the ones you need to know are

Jessie, James, and Meowth. They may seem funny or _____ at
_____ ADJECTIVE

first, but don't take their power _____! Jessie, with her long
_____ ADVERB

_____ and her _____-type Pokémon, is known for
PART OF THE BODY _____ NOUN

her _____ anger. James is a master of disguise, dressing up as
_____ ADJECTIVE

Professor Oak, _____, or even a bush or a/an _____!
_____ CELEBRITY _____ NOUN

Meowth wants to please his _____ boss, Giovanni, and will
_____ ADJECTIVE

_____ or steal Pokémon to do it. So, if you see a few
_____ VERB

_____ characters _____ around Pallet Town
ADJECTIVE _____ VERB ENDING IN "ING"

wearing a/an _____ uniform with a big red *R*, you know
_____ COLOR

you've encountered Team _____!
_____ NOUN

MAD LIBS® is fun to play with friends, but you can also play it by yourself! To begin with, DO NOT look at the story on the page below. Fill in the blanks on this page with the words called for. Then, using the words you have selected, fill in the blank spaces in the story.

Now you've created your own hilarious MAD LIBS® game!

TRAVEL GUIDE TO THE ALOLA REGION

ADJECTIVE _____

NOUN _____

VERB ENDING IN "ING" _____

ADJECTIVE _____

ADVERB _____

PLURAL NOUN _____

PLURAL NOUN _____

PLURAL NOUN _____

ADJECTIVE _____

VERB _____

VERB _____

NOUN _____

ADVERB _____

CELEBRITY _____

ADJECTIVE _____

ADJECTIVE _____

PLURAL NOUN _____

MAD LIBS®
TRAVEL GUIDE TO THE ALOLA REGION

Thank you for visiting the _____ Alola region, a/an
                              ADJECTIVE
_____ that has something for everyone. It's not a nearby
    NOUN
region, but it's perfect for relaxing in the sun or _____
                                                VERB ENDING IN "ING"
new Pokémon. Alola is a group of tropical, _____ islands
                                                ADJECTIVE
where humans and Pokémon live _____ together. In fact, all
                                   ADVERB
_____ of transportation are powered by Pokémon! Alola is
  PLURAL NOUN
home to the Pokémon School, a place where Pokémon and
_____ study together. Surrounded by slides, a racecourse,
  PLURAL NOUN
pools, the ocean, and _____, there is always something
                          PLURAL NOUN
_____ to do or _____. If you are here to
  ADJECTIVE   VERB
_____ Pokémon, you have a hard _____ ahead of
    VERB   NOUN
you. A Grand Trial is _____ difficult. Usually you have to face
                          ADVERB
an Island Kahuna such as _____, which is never
                              CELEBRITY
_____! We hope you enjoy your stay in the Alola region,
  ADJECTIVE
where _____ sights and difficult _____ await!
          ADJECTIVE   PLURAL NOUN

MAD LIBS® is fun to play with friends, but you can also play it by yourself! To begin with, DO NOT look at the story on the page below. Fill in the blanks on this page with the words called for. Then, using the words you have selected, fill in the blank spaces in the story.

Now you've created your own hilarious MAD LIBS® game!

BATTLING IN A POKÉMON LEAGUE TOURNAMENT

NOUN _____

PLURAL NOUN _____

VERB _____

ADVERB _____

ADJECTIVE _____

VERB _____

ADJECTIVE _____

NUMBER _____

VERB ENDING IN "ING" _____

PLURAL NOUN _____

VERB _____

VERB ENDING IN "ING" _____

ADJECTIVE _____

PLURAL NOUN _____

NOUN _____

ADJECTIVE _____

A PLACE _____

MAD LIBS
BATTLING IN A POKÉMON LEAGUE TOURNAMENT

If you've already registered for a region's Pokémon _____ and

NOUN

collected at least eight _____, it's time to _____ a

PLURAL NOUN · · · · · · · · · · · · · · · · · · VERB

Pokémon League Tournament. Never do this _____, though.

ADVERB

After the _____ opening ceremony, the qualifying rounds

ADJECTIVE

begin. This is to _____ out the Trainers who are not yet ready

VERB

to compete. Then, Trainers must battle in the _____ preliminary

ADJECTIVE

rounds until there are only _____ Trainers left. After a short

NUMBER

break, the real _____ begins! The final _____

VERB ENDING IN "ING" · · · · · · · · · · · · PLURAL NOUN

are Full Battles with six Pokémon on each side. _____ them

VERB

carefully, because it may mean winning or _____ the

VERB ENDING IN "ING"

Tournament! Depending on where you are, the terrain could be

_____. You could encounter ice, rocks, and even

ADJECTIVE

_____! But winning a/an _____ is only the

PLURAL NOUN · · · · · · · · · · · · · · · NOUN

beginning. After that comes the _____ Elite Four . . . and

ADJECTIVE

eventually Champion of (the) _____!

A PLACE

MAD LIBS® is fun to play with friends, but you can also play it by yourself! To begin with, DO NOT look at the story on the page below. Fill in the blanks on this page with the words called for. Then, using the words you have selected, fill in the blank spaces in the story.

Now you've created your own hilarious MAD LIBS® game!

APPROACHING WILD POKÉMON

VERB _____

ADJECTIVE _____

NOUN _____

ADVERB _____

VERB _____

A PLACE _____

ADJECTIVE _____

VERB ENDING IN "ING" _____

ADJECTIVE _____

VERB _____

ADJECTIVE _____

VERB _____

ADJECTIVE _____

VERB _____

MAD☺LIBS®
APPROACHING WILD POKÉMON

Wild Pokémon are rare to come across, but if you do _____
                                                        VERB

one, it's best to be _____ and prepared. Some Pokémon want
                        ADJECTIVE

to be left alone, but sometimes they want the _____ of other
                                                  NOUN

Pokémon and _____ wish to be caught and trained. In order
                 ADVERB

to catch a wild Pokémon, first you have to find and _____
                                                        VERB

one. They often live outside a city or (the) _____, and can be
                                                A PLACE

found in the grass or in the _____ water. Sometimes they are
                                ADJECTIVE

out in the open, but sometimes they are _____ in a
                                          VERB ENDING IN "ING"

hollow stump or in a/an _____ cave. But _____
                            ADJECTIVE   VERB

them carefully—wild Pokémon can be _____. Often, this
                                        ADJECTIVE

leads to a battle. Choose a Pokémon who you feel will _____
                                                          VERB

best for you and let it loose. When you feel the wild Pokémon is

_____ enough, toss a Poké Ball and see if you _____ it!
   ADJECTIVE   VERB

From POKÉMON MAD LIBS® • © 2017 The Pokémon Company International.
TM, ® Nintendo. Published by Mad Libs, an imprint of Penguin Random House LLC.

MAD LIBS® is fun to play with friends, but you can also play it by yourself! To begin with, DO NOT look at the story on the page below. Fill in the blanks on this page with the words called for. Then, using the words you have selected, fill in the blank spaces in the story.

Now you've created your own hilarious MAD LIBS® game!

YOUR POKÉ BALL AND YOU

COLOR _____

NOUN _____

PART OF THE BODY _____

PLURAL NOUN _____

ARTICLE OF CLOTHING _____

ADJECTIVE _____

VERB _____

VERB ENDING IN "ING" _____

VERB _____

NOUN _____

VERB _____

NOUN _____

NOUN _____

VERB _____

VERB ENDING IN "ING" _____

MAD LIBS®

YOUR POKÉ BALL AND YOU

What's red and _____, as round as a/an _____, and
 COLOR   NOUN

fits in the palm of your _____? A Poké Ball, of course! No
                          PART OF THE BODY

Trainer would be caught without a few _____ in their
                                       PLURAL NOUN

backpack or in their _____. You never know when
                      ARTICLE OF CLOTHING

you might come across a/an _____ Pokémon that you need
                            ADJECTIVE

to _____. If you are _____ a Pokémon and
   VERB   VERB ENDING IN "ING"

weaken it enough, you can try to _____ it. Just throw your
                                  VERB

Poké Ball. The _____ might escape, but if it fails, the
               NOUN

Pokémon is captured, ready to train. Then it will _____ for
                                                   VERB

you whenever you like. Just toss your Poké Ball at your _____.
                                                         NOUN

In a flash of _____, your Pokémon will be ready to
               NOUN

_____ and fight! So, stock up on Poké Balls and start
VERB

_____ today!
VERB ENDING IN "ING"

MAD LIBS® is fun to play with friends, but you can also play it by yourself! To begin with, DO NOT look at the story on the page below. Fill in the blanks on this page with the words called for. Then, using the words you have selected, fill in the blank spaces in the story.

Now you've created your own hilarious MAD LIBS® game!

PREPPING FOR YOUR POKÉMON ADVENTURE

A PLACE _____

VERB _____

ADJECTIVE _____

VERB _____

SILLY WORD _____

PLURAL NOUN _____

ADJECTIVE _____

PLURAL NOUN _____

ADJECTIVE _____

NOUN _____

ADVERB _____

ADJECTIVE _____

PLURAL NOUN _____

VERB _____

ADJECTIVE _____

MAD LIBS®
PREPPING FOR YOUR POKÉMON ADVENTURE

If you want to start traveling around (the) _____ catching
A PLACE

Pokémon, you'll need to _____ first. Here's a list of what
VERB

you'll need:

- **A backpack:** You can only carry _____ Poké Balls, so
  ADJECTIVE

  you'll need someplace to _____ all the others.
  VERB

- **Poké Balls:** Of course you need these! You wouldn't be able to

  catch Komala, Mimikyu, or _____ if you didn't have a
  SILLY WORD

  stash of _____ at the ready!
  PLURAL NOUN

- _____ **friends:** No one does well alone. Travel with
  ADJECTIVE

  _____ and you'll go much further. Where you are
  PLURAL NOUN

  weak, your friends can be _____.
  ADJECTIVE

- **A positive attitude:** One _____ all Trainers share is they
  NOUN

  are _____ confident. You must have _____
  ADVERB   ADJECTIVE

  strength if you want to win a Gym battle and earn _____.
  PLURAL NOUN

So, good luck on your quest to catch and _____ Pokémon. It
VERB

is a difficult life, but a/an _____ one!
ADJECTIVE

From POKÉMON MAD LIBS® • © 2017 The Pokémon Company International.
TM, ® Nintendo. Published by Mad Libs, an imprint of Penguin Random House LLC.

MAD LIBS® is fun to play with friends, but you can also play it by yourself! To begin with, DO NOT look at the story on the page below. Fill in the blanks on this page with the words called for. Then, using the words you have selected, fill in the blank spaces in the story.

Now you've created your own hilarious MAD LIBS® game!

IDEA FOR A NEW POKÉMON CONTEST ROUND

ADJECTIVE _____

VERB _____

ADVERB _____

VERB _____

NUMBER _____

VERB ENDING IN "ING" _____

NOUN _____

ADJECTIVE _____

VERB _____

ADJECTIVE _____

PLURAL NOUN _____

NOUN _____

NOUN _____

ADJECTIVE _____

MAD LIBS
IDEA FOR A NEW POKÉMON
CONTEST ROUND

Everyone knows there are two rounds in a Pokémon Contest: the

Performance Stage and the _____ Battle Stage. In the
ADJECTIVE

Performance Stage, the Trainer must _____ their Pokémon in
VERB

order to appeal to the judges. That means using your Pokémon as

creatively and _____ as possible. Then, of course, there's the
ADVERB

Battle Stage, where two Trainers _____ each other for _____
VERB NUMBER

minutes. Trainers are scored for winning, for _____ new
VERB ENDING IN "ING"

moves, and even for just a successful _____. But I think there
NOUN

should be a third—even more _____—round. It would be
ADJECTIVE

called the Speed Stage. The Trainer must _____ their Pokémon
VERB

through a complex and _____ obstacle course. You can use
ADJECTIVE

moves and _____ to speed your Pokémon along, and
PLURAL NOUN

scoring is based on time and _____. It would add a whole
NOUN

new _____ to a Pokémon Contest, and it would be
NOUN

_____ to watch!
ADJECTIVE

MAD LIBS® is fun to play with friends, but you can also play it by yourself! To begin with, DO NOT look at the story on the page below. Fill in the blanks on this page with the words called for. Then, using the words you have selected, fill in the blank spaces in the story.

Now you've created your own hilarious MAD LIBS® game!

BEWARE OF MEWTWO

ADJECTIVE _____

NOUN _____

VERB ENDING IN "ING" _____

ADJECTIVE _____

PERSON IN ROOM _____

NOUN _____

VERB _____

SAME VERB _____

ADJECTIVE _____

ADJECTIVE _____

PLURAL NOUN _____

PLURAL NOUN _____

VERB _____

ADJECTIVE _____

VERB _____

MAD LIBS

BEWARE OF MEWTWO

Mewtwo is an interesting but _____ addition to the Pokémon
ADJECTIVE

_____. Created after years of gene _____ and
NOUN VERB ENDING IN "ING"

experiments, this _____ Psychic-type Pokémon (along with
ADJECTIVE

_____) may be related to Mew, a Pokémon said to have cells
PERSON IN ROOM

that contain the entirety of the _____ genetic code. Mewtwo has
NOUN

never been seen to _____ into any other forms, but it can
VERB

_____ into the _____ Mega Mewtwo. It is said Mewtwo
SAME VERB ADJECTIVE

has the most savage and _____ heart of all Pokémon and
ADJECTIVE

lives only to defeat its _____. Mewtwo is capable of
PLURAL NOUN

levitation, telepathy, and _____, and other Pokémon
PLURAL NOUN

_____ at the thought of encountering it in the wild. It is said
VERB

that this Pokémon now lives in deep, _____ caves.
ADJECTIVE

All I can say is: If you see a Mewtwo coming your way, turn around

and _____!
VERB

MAD LIBS® is fun to play with friends, but you can also play it by yourself! To begin with, DO NOT look at the story on the page below. Fill in the blanks on this page with the words called for. Then, using the words you have selected, fill in the blank spaces in the story.

Now you've created your own hilarious MAD LIBS® game!

ALL ABOUT POKÉMON GYMS

VERB _____

ADJECTIVE _____

PLURAL NOUN _____

VERB _____

VERB _____

ADVERB _____

VERB ENDING IN "ING" _____

VERB _____

VERB _____

NOUN _____

A PLACE _____

VERB _____

ADVERB _____

ADJECTIVE _____

MAD LIBS
ALL ABOUT
POKÉMON GYMS

A Gym is a place where Trainers _____ their Pokémon in
<small>VERB</small>

order to get them _____ and gain _____. Just like
<small>ADJECTIVE</small>   <small>PLURAL NOUN</small>

a regular gym, the more you _____ at a Gym, the stronger your
<small>VERB</small>

Pokémon will get. Trainers can _____ their own skills there,
<small>VERB</small>

too! If you want to be a Gym Leader, you need to be _____
<small>ADVERB</small>

skillful at battling with Pokémon, or at least at _____.
<small>VERB ENDING IN "ING"</small>

_____ eight badges and you can enter a League Conference.
<small>VERB</small>

It's the only way to _____ the respect and _____ of
<small>VERB</small>   <small>NOUN</small>

other Trainers. But know this: There is only one _____ in
<small>A PLACE</small>

each city, so you may have to _____ far and _____
<small>VERB</small>   <small>ADVERB</small>

to win enough Gym badges. But it's the only way for a Trainer to

become more _____!
<small>ADJECTIVE</small>

MAD LIBS® is fun to play with friends, but you can also play it by yourself! To begin with, DO NOT look at the story on the page below. Fill in the blanks on this page with the words called for. Then, using the words you have selected, fill in the blank spaces in the story.

Now you've created your own hilarious MAD LIBS® game!

PROFESSOR OAK, POKÉMON EXPERT

PLURAL NOUN _____

A PLACE _____

NOUN _____

PLURAL NOUN _____

OCCUPATION _____

COLOR _____

ARTICLE OF CLOTHING _____

PLURAL NOUN _____

VERB ENDING IN "ING" _____

PLURAL NOUN _____

ADJECTIVE _____

VERB ENDING IN "ING" _____

OCCUPATION _____

NOUN _____

NOUN _____

MAD LIBS®
PROFESSOR OAK,
POKÉMON EXPERT

When you think of Ash Ketchum's closest _____, it's easy

PLURAL NOUN

to list his traveling companions, but let's not forget about Professor

Oak! Professor Oak lives in (the) _____, where he has his

A PLACE

research lab. It is powered by a huge _____ that spins in the

NOUN

breeze! Professor Oak is one of Ash's first _____ in his quest

PLURAL NOUN

to become the greatest Pokémon _____. Dressed in a

OCCUPATION

standard _____ lab coat and _____, he spends

COLOR ARTICLE OF CLOTHING

his days and _____ researching and _____

PLURAL NOUN VERB ENDING IN "ING"

Pokémon to help others reach their goals and _____.

PLURAL NOUN

Even though he's often _____, Professor Oak knows almost

ADJECTIVE

everything there is to know about Pokémon and does a great job

_____ them for his friends. Professor Oak may not be

VERB ENDING IN "ING"

out there battling a Trainer or a/an _____, but he has been

OCCUPATION

Ash's biggest ally and _____. Go Professor _____!

NOUN NOUN

MAD LIBS® is fun to play with friends, but you can also play it by yourself! To begin with, DO NOT look at the story on the page below. Fill in the blanks on this page with the words called for. Then, using the words you have selected, fill in the blank spaces in the story.

Now you've created your own hilarious MAD LIBS® game!

IF TEAM ROCKET STOLE MY POKÉMON

NOUN _____

NOUN _____

VERB (PAST TENSE) _____

ADJECTIVE _____

ADJECTIVE _____

VERB _____

ADJECTIVE _____

PERSON IN ROOM _____

VERB _____

PLURAL NOUN _____

ADJECTIVE _____

VERB _____

MAD LIBS®
IF TEAM ROCKET STOLE MY POKÉMON

If I was minding my own _____, wandering through Pallet

NOUN

Town, and Team Rocket jumped out from behind a/an _____

NOUN

and _____ my Snorlax, I'd be so _____! Normally,

VERB (PAST TENSE)   ADJECTIVE

I'd take my time getting my Pokémon back, but Snorlax was one

of my first Pokémon ever. Plus, he's so soft and _____! I'd

ADJECTIVE

_____ after them right away. I'd throw every Poké Ball I

VERB

owned and get Gyarados, Bewear, and even the _____

ADJECTIVE

Magikarp in the battle. I know it would be a lot, taking on Jessie,

_____, and Meowth all at once, but I wouldn't want Team

PERSON IN ROOM

Rocket to think they could _____ me around. Anyhow, I'd want

VERB

Snorlax back so badly! A mixture of anger and _____ would

PLURAL NOUN

make me battle harder until all of Team Rocket and their whole

_____ School was left in rubble. I _____ you, Snorlax!

ADJECTIVE   VERB

MAD LIBS® is fun to play with friends, but you can also play it by yourself! To begin with, DO NOT look at the story on the page below. Fill in the blanks on this page with the words called for. Then, using the words you have selected, fill in the blank spaces in the story.

Now you've created your own hilarious MAD LIBS® game!

SOME OF ASH'S FRIENDS

NOUN _____

ADJECTIVE _____

PLURAL NOUN _____

VERB (PAST TENSE) _____

PLURAL NOUN _____

ADJECTIVE _____

NOUN _____

A PLACE _____

VERB (PAST TENSE) _____

PLURAL NOUN _____

A PLACE _____

VERB ENDING IN "ING" _____

ADJECTIVE _____

OCCUPATION _____

ADJECTIVE _____

ADJECTIVE _____

PLURAL NOUN _____

MAD LIBS

SOME OF ASH'S FRIENDS

Although Ash started his _____ alone, he has made many
                        NOUN

_____ friends along the way. One of his first _____
ADJECTIVE   PLURAL NOUN

was Misty. Ash _____ her after his Pikachu damaged
               VERB (PAST TENSE)

her bike, but then they became the best of _____. She is
                                            PLURAL NOUN

the Gym Leader of the _____ Cerulean Gym and specializes
                      ADJECTIVE

in _____-type Pokémon. Ash met Brock after they battled in
   NOUN

(the) _____. They _____ together for many
      A PLACE   VERB (PAST TENSE)

_____, through Kanto, Johto, and all the way to (the)
PLURAL NOUN

_____ until _____ ways. Brock's _____
A PLACE   VERB ENDING IN "ING"   ADJECTIVE

Pokémon was Onix, and Brock wants to be a Pokémon _____!
                                                   OCCUPATION

More recently, Ash has teamed up with Clemont, genius of Electric-

type Pokémon, and the _____ Serena. Just look at her
                      ADJECTIVE

_____ hat! No matter what, one thing's for sure—Ash would
ADJECTIVE

never have gotten this far without his _____!
                                       PLURAL NOUN

From POKÉMON MAD LIBS® • © 2017 The Pokémon Company International.
TM, ® Nintendo. Published by Mad Libs, an imprint of Penguin Random House LLC.

MAD LIBS® is fun to play with friends, but you can also play it by yourself! To begin with, DO NOT look at the story on the page below. Fill in the blanks on this page with the words called for. Then, using the words you have selected, fill in the blank spaces in the story.

Now you've created your own hilarious MAD LIBS® game!

SQUIRTLE, SO CUTE

ADJECTIVE _____

NOUN _____

NOUN _____

NOUN _____

ADJECTIVE _____

NOUN _____

ADJECTIVE _____

VERB _____

PLURAL NOUN _____

NOUN _____

PLURAL NOUN _____

ADJECTIVE _____

TYPE OF LIQUID _____

OCCUPATION _____

NOUN _____

ADVERB _____

MAD LIBS®

SQUIRTLE, SO CUTE

What's blue, _____, covered in a hard _____, and
       ADJECTIVE   NOUN

probably the cutest _____ you've ever seen? Squirtle, of course!
                  NOUN

Although it's uncommon in the _____, Squirtle are one of
                           NOUN

the Pokémon many Kanto-region Trainers start their adventures with

(along with Bulbasaur and the _____ Charmander). Squirtle
                     ADJECTIVE

like to gather in groups near the _____ or on _____
                        NOUN   ADJECTIVE

islands. Like many other Water-type Pokémon, Squirtle love to

_____ Torrent when they are in battle. But they also have
  VERB

other _____ up their sleeves. For example, a Squirtle's
      PLURAL NOUN

shell is a useful _____. It can pull into it for defense or for
            NOUN

_____, and its ridges allow Squirtle to be _____
  PLURAL NOUN   ADJECTIVE

underwater. A Squirtle can spray _____ from its mouth
                  TYPE OF LIQUID

with great accuracy. If you don't watch out, you'll get a face full of it!

So, if you want to be a great Pokémon _____, be sure to have
                      OCCUPATION

a Squirtle in your _____! You'll be _____ glad you did.
         NOUN   ADVERB

MAD LIBS® is fun to play with friends, but you can also play it by yourself! To begin with, DO NOT look at the story on the page below. Fill in the blanks on this page with the words called for. Then, using the words you have selected, fill in the blank spaces in the story.

Now you've created your own hilarious MAD LIBS® game!

STAY AWAY FROM TEAM SKULL!

PLURAL NOUN _____

ADJECTIVE _____

VERB ENDING IN "ING" _____

PLURAL NOUN _____

NOUN _____

PLURAL NOUN _____

ADJECTIVE _____

COLOR _____

PART OF THE BODY _____

VERB _____

ADVERB _____

PERSON IN ROOM _____

ADJECTIVE _____

VERB _____

ADJECTIVE _____

VEHICLE _____

VERB ENDING IN "ING" _____

NOUN _____

MAD LIBS®
STAY AWAY FROM TEAM SKULL!

Who are those nasty _____ bothering everyone else around
_{PLURAL NOUN}

them? Team Skull, of course. They may seem cool or _____ at
_{ADJECTIVE}

first, but they're not! Seen _____ around the Alola
_{VERB ENDING IN "ING"}

Islands on motorcycles, this gang of _____ is always
_{PLURAL NOUN}

looking for a/an _____. They bully Trainers into _____
_{NOUN}   _{PLURAL NOUN}

and then take away their favorite Pokémon. It's _____ to spot
_{ADJECTIVE}

them. Each member wears a black-and-_____ T-shirt and a
_{COLOR}

bandana over his or her _____. Members of Team Skull only
_{PART OF THE BODY}

_____ when they know they're going to _____ win.
_{VERB}   _{ADVERB}

That's why Ash, _____, and their _____ friends
_{PERSON IN ROOM}   _{ADJECTIVE}

need to _____ together. So, if you're _____, you'll stay
_{VERB}   _{ADJECTIVE}

away from anyone riding a/an _____ and _____
_{VEHICLE}   _{VERB ENDING IN "ING"}

a black-and-white outfit. Beware of Team _____!
_{NOUN}

From POKÉMON MAD LIBS® • © 2017 The Pokémon Company International.
TM, ® Nintendo. Published by Mad Libs, an imprint of Penguin Random House LLC.

MAD LIBS® is fun to play with friends, but you can also play it by yourself! To begin with, DO NOT look at the story on the page below. Fill in the blanks on this page with the words called for. Then, using the words you have selected, fill in the blank spaces in the story.

Now you've created your own hilarious MAD LIBS® game!

TEAM ROCKET ARE AMATEURS!

ADJECTIVE _____

ADJECTIVE _____

PLURAL NOUN _____

PLURAL NOUN _____

NOUN _____

A PLACE _____

COLOR _____

ARTICLE OF CLOTHING (PLURAL) _____

VERB _____

ADJECTIVE _____

PLURAL NOUN _____

A PLACE _____

ADJECTIVE _____

ADJECTIVE _____

PLURAL NOUN _____

MAD●LIBS®
TEAM ROCKET ARE AMATEURS!

Sure, Team Rocket thinks they are so _____ with their
 ADJECTIVE

_____ outfits and fancy _____. But if I were the
 ADJECTIVE   PLURAL NOUN

boss of a team of _____, we'd be the best. First of all, we'd
                   PLURAL NOUN

be called Team _____ and our headquarters would be (the)
                NOUN

_____. We would all wear _____ armor and have the
 A PLACE   COLOR

coolest _____. Our sworn goal would be to
         ARTICLE OF CLOTHING (PLURAL)

_____ new Pokémon by exploring the farthest parts of the
 VERB

world. Who knows what kind of _____ Pokémon we'd see, or
                               ADJECTIVE

how many _____ we'd find in the strangest of places. We
          PLURAL NOUN

would travel to the bottom of the ocean or even to (the) _____
                                                          A PLACE

if we thought we could find an undiscovered and _____
                                                 ADJECTIVE

Pokémon. We'd make lots of _____ hard cash, too. And we
                            ADJECTIVE

would never let Ash Ketchum or any of his _____ stand in
                                           PLURAL NOUN

our way!

From POKÉMON MAD LIBS® • © 2017 The Pokémon Company International.
TM, ® Nintendo. Published by Mad Libs, an imprint of Penguin Random House LLC.

MAD LIBS® is fun to play with friends, but you can also play it by yourself! To begin with, DO NOT look at the story on the page below. Fill in the blanks on this page with the words called for. Then, using the words you have selected, fill in the blank spaces in the story.

Now you've created your own hilarious MAD LIBS® game!

BECOMING LEAGUE CHAMPION

PLURAL NOUN _____

ADVERB _____

VERB ENDING IN "ING" _____

ADJECTIVE _____

NOUN _____

VERB _____

NOUN _____

PLURAL NOUN _____

NOUN _____

NOUN _____

OCCUPATION _____

ADJECTIVE _____

NOUN _____

ADJECTIVE _____

PERSON IN ROOM _____

A PLACE _____

So, you've completed the Pokémon League, collected your eight

_____ , and _____ defeated the Elite Four . . . It's
PLURAL NOUN   ADVERB

time to think about _____ the League Champion.
                    VERB ENDING IN "ING"

The _____ work begins now! Pokémon League Champion
    ADJECTIVE

(also known as a League _____) is the highest rank a Pokémon
                        NOUN

Trainer can _____. You will have the respect and _____
            VERB   NOUN

of other Trainers and enjoy all the _____ your region has to
                                    PLURAL NOUN

offer—including your own Champion's _____! But beware,
                                    NOUN

other Trainers will now be looking to take your _____ from
                                                NOUN

you. If you lose to another _____, you must give your
                            OCCUPATION

_____ _____ to them (unless they don't want it).
ADJECTIVE   NOUN

Notable Champions include the _____ Cynthia (Sinnoh
                              ADJECTIVE

region), Diantha (Kalos region), and _____
                                     PERSON IN ROOM

([the] _____). Do you think you have what it takes to be a
       A PLACE

Pokémon League Champion? Go for it!